# The ABC's of Salvation

Your Handbook to Salvation,
False Doctrine, and Overcoming
the Mental Illness that Prevents Faith

Spencer Doris

Copyright © 2011 by Spencer Doris

*The ABC's of Salvation*
*Your Handbook to Salvation, False Doctrine, and Overcoming the Mental Illness that Prevents Faith*
by Spencer Doris

Printed in the United States of America

ISBN 9781619040359
Library of Congress Control Number: 2010914856

All rights reserved solely by the author. The author guarantees all contents are original and do not infringe upon the legal rights of any other person or work. No part of this book may be reproduced in any form without the permission of the author. The views expressed in this book are not necessarily those of the publisher.

Unless otherwise indicated, Bible quotations are taken from The Holy Bible, New International Version, NIV. Copyright © 1973, 1978, 1984, 2011 by Biblica Inc. TM Used by Permission of Zondervan. All rights reserved worldwide. www.zondervan.com The NIV and "New International Version" are trademarks registered in the United States Patent and Trademark Office by Biblica, Inc. TM.

www.xulonpress.com

# Contents

Introduction ................................................................. ix

Chapter 1
Who is guilty of breaking God's laws? ....................... 11

Chapter 2
What is God's definition of sin? ................................... 17

Chapter 3
What are the results, consequences,
and punishments of sin? ............................................... 21

Chapter 4
Does God save us because we do good deeds
or good works? .............................................................. 29

Chapter 5
What was the free gift? ................................................. 33

Chapter 6
How do I receive the free gift? ..................................... 36

Chapter 7
What is the process of one becoming a true Christian? ......... 42

*The ABC's of Salvation*

Chapter 8
    What is the proof of my salvation? ............................................51

Chapter 9
    What is proof that I might not be saved? ...............................54

Chapter 10
    Can I still be saved when I have mental illness
    and can't understand what I am reading? ...............................60

Chapter 11
    Staying Saved! .......................................................................69

Chapter 12
    Finding the Right Church ......................................................74

Chapter 13
    What are a few false teachings about salvation? ....................81

# *Dedication*

*I* would like to dedicate this book to all the mentally handicapped out there who want to get healed from their illness. I know it won't be easy getting healed from your disease. It has been the most difficult challenge I've ever faced but I know once I have overcome it, I will be the most blessed person I know. I have had some signs of improvement, which have led to brokenness, and have felt loved by God at times, where for the last fifteen years I have felt like God has hated me. But I want you to know that once you are free from your illness, you will feel more loved by God than you can imagine, and you will be extremely grateful once it's over with, not to mention you will get to spend an eternity with God and his family. Stay strong and persevere even if there is no one to help you. To everyone out there who isn't mentally handicapped, I plead with you to help those who are mentally challenged to get better. Serve them and help them to get detoxified because it is very difficult to do this by yourself, and love them and don't judge them. I would also like to dedicate this book to God and Jesus for giving up everything for me.

# Introduction

Over the years, I have wondered whether or not I was saved. I was always afraid of dying. I had an accused and guilty conscience over sin. But I read in the Bible that I shouldn't feel guilty anymore once I am saved; instead, maybe I should be broken, and my conscience should be cleansed. I read that I should have an inexpressible and glorious joy if I were saved. For so many years, I studied the topic of salvation, and once I figured it out, I realized I needed a sharp and intelligent mind in order to be saved by faith and I didn't have that because of a disease I had called Attention-Deficit Disorder. I then started working on the problem that caused my mental health problems, which was a combination of heavy metal poisoning and vitamin and mineral deficiencies that I received from the toxic metals in my amalgam dental fillings and aluminum soda cans. Once I realized this, I had all my fillings removed and began to detoxify myself to better health, and now I am writing you to let you know what it takes to become a true Christian, how to recognize false doctrine and false teachers, and how to remain a Christian. As you read this book please do not harden your hearts, but study it out on your own to see if it is true. God bless you as you read this book.

# Chapter 1

# Who is guilty of breaking God's laws?

The first question we must ask ourselves today is "If I am a good person, will I go to heaven?" The second question we should ask ourselves is "Have I actually sinned or broken any of God's laws?" Third is "Am I a sinner or a slave to sin?"

One of the common misconceptions of society is people generally believe that they are good. I have heard people say they are going to heaven because they believe they are good. We must ask ourselves "Is that a true statement?" First, we must ask ourselves what is the truth and how do know it's the truth. The scripture is the truth. In **2 Timothy 3:16** it says *"Every scripture inspired of God is also profitable for teaching, for reproof, for correction, for instruction which is in righteousness"* (American Standard Version). The way we know scripture is the truth is we test it with other bible verses and make sure they back each other up and we use our mind in the state it is supposed to be in to discern truth, which means we need excellent mental health and sharpness to discern truth in its purest form. So back to the question are people actually good. In **Mark 10:17-19**, it says, *"And as he was going forth into the way, there ran one to him, and kneeled to him, and asked him, Good Teacher, what shall I do that I may inherit eternal life? And Jesus said unto him, Why callest thou me good? none is good save one, even God. Thou knowest the commandments, Do not kill, Do not commit adultery, Do not steal, Do not bear false witness, Do not defraud, Honor thy* *father and mother'" (American Standard Version)* So we see, Jesus sets the standard to judge us by and that was the law and the Ten Commandments. He also says no one is good except God, so that eliminates the whole world to being good.

So basically, the law was what God gave his people through Moses, which encompassed all the rules and regulations that were there to show the people how to live. The law might have been there to show us how to live, but it wasn't there to bring us eternal life. It states in **Galatians 3:21** *"Is the law, therefore, opposed to the promises of God? Absolutely not! For if a law had been given that could impart life, then righteousness would certainly have come by the law."* (NIV)

What part of the law did the Israelites and other characters in the Bible believe would justify them? (Justify just basically means would make them right with God.) These Jews believed that they were justified through the Levitical priesthood. This was the old part of the law that stated that animal sacrifices had to be made in order to pay the penalty of sins in each Israelite's life. It also says in Galatians and Romans that no one will be justified by the law. Again that part of the law that people were trying to be justified by was the animal sacrifices.

Another part of the law that the Israelites might have been trying to be justified by was just trying to obey everything written in the law. It is difficult to tell at least from the New Testament what these men were trying to do to justify themselves. Maybe it was loving the Lord with all of the heart, maybe it was loving their neighbor as themselves, maybe it was giving to the poor, and finally, it could have been trying to obey everything written in the entire law. It could have been a number of other good actions too. I kind of believe it's the good deeds that people were trying to do that they thought made them right with God and the animal sacrifices. Some of the verses that would be good to study on your own would be **Deuteronomy 6:1-25** and focus on **verse 25**. Also another good chapter would be **Acts 15**. In **Galatians 5:3** and **Galatian 3:10-13** talking about people trying to obey everything written in the law. The Israelites were trying to get there righteousness from the works of law.

We must ask ourselves, "If we aren't justified by the law then what was its purpose?" There are a couple purposes of the Mosaic Law. In **Romans 3:20**, it says, *"Therefore no one will be declared righteous in God's sight by the works of the law; rather, through the law we become conscious of our sin."* (NIV) So the law was put there to show us that we have sin not to make us right with God through the animal sacrifices or through good deeds or works. It is made clear in **Galatians 5:3-4** *"Again I declare to every man who lets himself be circumcised that he is obligated to obey the whole law. You who are trying to be justified by the law have been alienated from Christ; you have fallen away from grace."* (NIV) Why does it say they were alienated from Christ in **Galatians 5:3**? Because Christ was the true sacrifice that forgives sin, and these people were putting their trust in the animal sacrifices and taking their trust out of Christ's sacrifice. They were also putting their trust in their obedience to the law instead Christ paying the penalty.

So when you obligate yourself to obey the whole law in order to be right with God then you have fallen from grace or have fallen from the free gift. Also, whenever we see the words justified by observing the law or justified by law, it often means as justified by "works or actions of the law." One of the scriptures that talk about what the people thought might justify them was in **Hebrews 10:4**: *"It is impossible for the blood of bulls and goats to take away sins."* (NIV) This scripture shows us that the Israelites thought that the animal sacrifices were able to take away sin. But the writer of Hebrews teaches us that it was impossible for these sacrifices to take away sin. In fact these sacrifices were just a reminder of sin because it didn't wash the believer's conscience, which in turn was showing them they needed to wait for a better sacrifice than the animal sacrifices.

We must also ask ourselves what was another purpose of the law; it says in **Hebrews 10:1**, *"The law is only a shadow of the good things that are coming—not the realities themselves. For this reason it can never, by the same sacrifices repeated endlessly year after year, make perfect those who draw near to worship."* (NIV)

Now we must ask ourselves what this means. It means that the Old Testament Law was a shadow or an outline of how Christians are supposed to live but without the animal sacrifices. For example, the law has a lot of guidelines and rules about what to do and what not to do if we are to live a life pleasing to God. It also has the animal sacrifices that are a foreshadow of Jesus being the final sacrifice to come. It's the same way with the New Testament; there is a bunch of rules that God would like us to follow if we are going to remain in God's love. In **John 15:10** Jesus says: *"If you keep my commands, you will remain in my love." (NIV)*

So in order to remain right with God we need to obey Jesus's teaching.

What else do we need to know about the law?

**Galatians 3:19** *"Why, then, was the law given at all? It was added because of transgressions."* (NIV) If the purpose of the law was to make us conscious of sin and to clearly state what the different sins are, and if its purpose wasn't to make us right with God through sacrifices or good works, then do we have scripture that also shows us that we all have sin. In **Romans 3:9-18**, it says,

*"What then? Are we better than they? No in no wise: for we have before proved both Jews and Gentiles, that they are all under sin; As it is written there is none righteous, no, not one: There is none that seeketh after God. They are all gone out of the way, they are together become unprofitable; there is none that doeth good, no not one. Their throat is an open sepulchre; with their tongues they have used deceit; the poison of asps under their lips: Whose mouth Is full of cursing and bitterness: Their feet Is swift to shed blood: Destruction and misery mark their ways: And the way of peace have they not known: There is no fear of God before their eyes."* (King James)

The next question we needed to ask ourselves is "Have I actually sinned or broken any of God's laws?" In **Romans 3:23**, it says, *"For all have sinned, and come short of the glory of God."* (King James) So that covers everyone; all have sinned. There are some people out there who don't even know they have sinned or broken any of God's laws. Because they don't know they have sinned, that is why the law was put out there, **Romans 3:20** *"rather, through the law we become conscious of our sin."* (NIV)

The third question we should ask ourselves is "Am I a slave of sin?" The scripture that covers this is in **Galatians 3:22**, it says, *"But the scriptures say that everyone is a slave to sin" (SD)* So from these verses, we can see that there is no one righteous, no one who does good, all have sinned, and the whole world is a slave of sin. The next chapter will go over the different sins just to let us know in what ways we have broken God's commands.

# Notes

# Chapter 2

# What is God's definition of sin?

How do we find out what sin is?

The first five books of the Bible are made up of the law. In **Romans 3:20**, it says, *"rather, through the law we become conscious of our sin."* (NIV) So the Old Testament Law and the Ten Commandments, which is part of the law, tell us what sin is and make us conscious of our sin. In **1 John 3:4**, it says, *"Everyone who sins breaks the law; in fact, sin is lawlessness."* (NIV) So this scripture tells us that sin is lawlessness, or sin is just a violation of breaking God's law.

There are also a number of scriptures in the New Testament that describe the different sins. In **Galatians 5:19-21** *"The acts of the flesh are obvious: sexual immorality, impurity and debauchery; idolatry and witchcraft; hatred, discord, jealousy, fits of rage, selfish ambition, dissensions, factions and envy; drunkenness, orgies, and the like. I warn you, as I did before, that those who live like this will not inherit the kingdom of God."* (NIV) When you get a chance you should really look up the definitions of these words to make sure you aren't living that way.

Another scripture that talks about sin is **Ephesians 5:3-5** *"But among you there must not be even a hint of sexual immorality, or of any kind of impurity, or of greed, because these are improper for*

*God's holy people. Nor should there be obscenity, foolish talk or coarse joking, which are out of place, but rather thanksgiving. For of this you can be sure: No immoral, impure or greedy person—such a person is an idolater—has any inheritance in the kingdom of Christ and of God."* (NIV) While in **Ephesians 4:29**, it says, *"Do not let any unwholesome talk come out of your mouths but only what is helpful for building others up according to their needs, that it may benefit those who listen."* (NIV)

In **Colossians 3:5-6** *"Put to death, therefore, whatever belongs to your earthly nature: sexual immorality, impurity, lust, evil desires and greed, which is idolatry. Because of these, the wrath of God is coming."* (NIV) In **Colossians 3:8-9** *"But now you must also rid yourselves of all such things as these: anger, rage, malice, slander, and filthy language from your lips. Do not lie to each other, since you have taken off your old self with its practices."* (NIV) The previous scriptures were taken out of the New Testament to help explain what the different sins are. There are also many other sin descriptions throughout the New Testament.

The following are a list of the Ten Commandments, and if you break one of these, then you have sinned and have then become a sinner.

**Exodus 20:2-17** *"I am Jehovah thy God, who brought thee out of the land of Egypt, out of the house of bondage."*

- *"Thou shalt have no other gods before me."*
- *"Thou shalt not make unto thee a graven image, nor any likeness of anything that is in heaven above, or that is the earth beneath, or that is in the water under the earth. Thou shalt not bow down thyself unto them, nor serve them, for I Jehovah thy God am a jealous God, visiting the iniquity of the fathers upon the children, upon the third and fourth generation of them who hate me and showing loving kindness unto thousands of them that love me and keep my commandments."*

- *"Thou shalt no take the name of Jehovah thy God in vain; for Jehovah will not hold him guiltless that taketh his name in vain."*
- *"Remember the sabbath day, to keep it holy. Six days shalt thou labor, and do all thy work; but the seventh day is a sabbath day unto Jehovah thy God: in it thou shalt not do any work, thou, nor thy son, nor thy daughter, thy man-servant, nor thy maid-servant, nor thy cattle, nor thy stranger that is within thy gates: for in six days Jehovah made heaven and earth, the sea, and all that in them is, and rested the seventh day: wherefore Jehovah blessed the sabbath day, and hallowed it."*
- *"Honor thy father and thy mother, that thy days may be long in the land which Jehovah thy God giveth thee."*
- *"Thou shalt not kill."*
- *"Thou shalt not commit adultery."*
- *"Thou shalt not steal."*
- *"Thou shalt not bear false witness against thy neighbor."*
- *"Thou shat not covet thy neighbors house, thou shalt not covet thy neighbors wife, nor his manservant, nor his maidservant, nor his ox, nor his 'donkey', nor anything that is thy neighbor's."* (American Standard)

Those were the Ten Commandments. A couple of them are clarified in the New Testament, being more specific as to what they mean. For example, committing adultery is specified in **Matthew 5:28** *"But I tell you that anyone who looks at a woman lustfully has already committed adultery with her in his heart."* (NIV) In **1 John 3:15** it says, *"Anyone who hates a brother or sister is a murderer, and you know that no murderer has eternal life residing in him."* (NIV) Basically, in the Old Testament, the first five books of the Bible are the Mosaic Law, and they go on to tell us about sin and how to live our lives. In the New Testament, God goes on to be more specific of what sin is. For a more in-depth study of sin and the law, just read the books of **Exodus**, **Leviticus**, **Numbers**, and **Deuteronomy** and also read all of the New Testament.

## Notes

# Chapter 3

# What are the results, consequences, and punishments of sin?

*Y*ou may ask yourself what is the big deal if I sin or not? I am not hurting anybody. But you see it is a big deal to God. One of the emotions God feels when he sees us sin is emotional pain. In **Genesis 6:5-6** *"The LORD saw how great the wickedness of the human race had become on the earth, and that every inclination of the thoughts of the human heart was only evil all the time. The LORD regretted that he had made human beings on the earth, and his heart was deeply troubled."* (NIV) It is also a big deal to everyone who has ever been hurt by someone else's sin. Has someone ever been hateful toward you? Has someone ever cheated on you? Has someone ever said an unkind word to you, or insulted you? The list goes on and on. The result of our sin is that these things hurt both God and man. God feels all the pain of every sin we have ever committed. I believe God has wept a lot because of all our sins.

Another result of our sin is God's emotion of anger and indignation. It says in **Romans 1:18** *"The wrath of God is being revealed from heaven against all the godlessness and wickedness of people, who suppress the truth by their wickedness,"* (NIV) So you see this scripture describes God as having wrath and the very definition of wrath encompasses anger and indignation and what is this that makes God angry. It is godlessness and wickedness.

What are some examples in the Old Testament of God's wrath?
**Genesis 19:1-5**

*"The two angels arrived at Sodom in the evening, and Lot was sitting in the gateway of the city. When he saw them, he got up to meet them and bowed down with his face to the ground. 'My lords,' he said, "please turn aside to your servant's house. You can wash your feet and spend the night and then go on your way early in the morning." 'No,' they answered, 'we will spend the night in the square.' But he insisted, so strongly that they did go with him and entered his house. He prepared a meal for them, baking bread without yeast, and they ate. Before they had gone to bed, all the men from every part of the city of Sodom—both young and old—surrounded the house. They called to Lot, "Where are the men who came to you tonight? Bring them out to us so that we can have sex with them." (NIV)*

In **Genesis 19:12-13**, *"And the men said unto Lot, 'Hast thou here any besides? son in law, and thy sons, and thy daughters, and whatsover thou hast In the city, bring them out of this place: For we will destroy this place, because the cry of them is waxen great before the face of the Lord and the Lord hath sent us to destroy it.'"* (King James) That is just one example of God's wrath in the Old Testament.

The second example of God's wrath in the Old Testament is found in **Genesis 6:5-8** *"And God saw that the wickedness of man was great in the earth, and that every imagination of the thoughts of his heart was only evil continually. And it repented the Lord that he had made man on the earth, and it grieved him at his heart. And the Lord said, I will destroy man whom I have created from the face of the earth; both man, and beast, and the creeping thing, and the fowls of the air; for It repenteth me that I have made them. But Noah found grace in the eyes of the Lord."* (King James) In **verse 11-13** *"The earth also was corrupt before God, and the earth was filled with violence. And God looked upon the earth, and, behold, it was* *corrupt; for all flesh had corrupted his way upon the earth. And God said unto Noah, The end of all flesh is come before me; for the earth is filled with violence through them; and, behold, I will destroy them with the earth.'"* (King James) In **Genesis 7:6** *"And Noah was six hundred years old when the flood was upon the earth."* (King James) This is the second example of God's wrath against mankind. There are many more examples in the Old Testament where God put to death individuals because they were wicked.

Where did these consequences of our sin begin, and what else were the consequences of our sin? **Genesis 3:17-19** *"And unto Adam he said, 'Because thou hast hearkened unto the voice of thy wife, and has eaten of the tree, of which I commanded thee, saying Thou shalt not eat of it: cursed is the ground for thy sake; in sorrow shalt not eat of it all the days of thy life; Thorns also and thistles shall bring it forth to thee; and thou shalt eat the herb of the field; In the sweat of thy face shalt eat bread, till thou return unto the ground; for out of it wast thou taken: for dust thou art, and unto dust shalt thou return.'"* (King James) So you see the ground is cursed. I believe the ground is cursed in more ways than one. One way the ground is cursed because we have terrible things happening in this world; for example, we have hurricanes, tornadoes, earthquakes. There wouldn't be disease in the world and people wouldn't be dying. So if you ever had a disease, you can blame it on the fact that the ground is cursed and it is cursed because man is being punished because of Adam and Eve's sin of eating from the tree.

What is another consequence of sin?
Ours sins put up a barrier between us and God so that we can't have a relationship with God. **Isaiah 59:1-2**
> *"Surely the arm of the Lord is not too short to save,*
> *nor his ear too dull to hear.*
> *But your iniquities have separated*
> *you from your God;*
> *your sins have hidden his face from you,*
> *so that he will not hear."* (NIV) Iniquities are just another word for sin.

What is punishment of not repenting of a sinful lifestyle after we die?

**Jude 1:7** *"Even as Sodom and Gomorrah and the cities about them in like manner, giving themselves over to fornication, and going after strange flesh, are set forth an example, suffering the vengeance of eternal fire."* (King James) According to this verse there is a punishment of eternal fire for those living like this.

**Matthew 25:45-46** *"Truly I tell you, whatever you did not do for one of the least of these, you did not do for me. Then they will go away to eternal punishment, but the righteous to eternal life."* (NIV) If you read this in context, (specifically in vs. 40 the bible uses the word brothers) you'll see that it tells us the importance of helping out our Christian brothers and sisters. So it is implying the importance of going to church so you can love your brothers and sisters in Christ, but if we are not going to church, we can't love our Christian brothers and sisters, which means like the verse says if you don't do things for the family of God you could be causing them to leave God because they don't have enough support as a Christian to make it and they fall away then you are partly to blame for them leaving God because you didn't love them and lay down your life for them. So basically I am saying that we go to church to encourage other believers and help and love the brothers and sisters to stay faithful. It talks about that in **Hebrews 3:12-13**. But back to **Matthew 25:45-46** it also is implying that you help out those that are strangers, basically people who are in need. Even if you didn't come to church maybe because you weren't able to, he would at least want you to come and meet with the family of believers on the other days. The following scriptures talk about that **Hebrews 10:25-26** *"Not forsaking the assembling of ourselves together, as the manner of some is; but exhorting one another: and so much the more, as ye see the day approaching. For if we sin wilfully after that we have received the knowledge of the truth, there remaineth no more sacrifice for sins."* (King James) According to this verse God would like us to meet all the more. The next verse that talks about us being plugged into the church is **John 15 vs. 4** *"Remain in* *me, as I also remain in you."* and in **vs. 5** *"apart from me you can do nothing."* (NIV) These verses basically explain that we need to remain is his church and his word and obey it to be saved **vs. 10** *"If you keep my commands, you will remain in my love, just as I have kept my Father's commands and remain in his love."*(NIV) I personally believe that you must remain in his body or the church to be saved, just read **John 15** where it talks about remaining in the vine. It also says we must obey him to remain in his love. If we aren't obeying him which includes going to church like **Hebrews 10:25** says then we aren't remaining in his love. There are many consequences to leaving the church. One thing that happens when we leave the church is we are more likely to go back to our sinful nature. Another thing that happens is we can get a seared conscience. When aren't exhorting one another daily like **Hebrews 3:13** says we get hardened or stubborn hearts and we stop repenting of our sin and then we lose our salvation. So the church is there to help us not go back to our sinful nature through encouragement and exhorting one another daily.

Now back to the punishments of sin. **Matthew 18:8** says, *"If your hand or your foot causes you to stumble, cut it off and throw it away. It is better for you to enter life maimed or crippled than to have two hands or two feet and be thrown into eternal fire."* (NIV) This scripture is obviously not talking about one sin here and there, but it is basically saying we need to do whatever we can to repent of our sinful nature. Finally, it is saying that there is a punishment of eternal fire for those who don't repent of a sin or a sinful lifestyle or nature. You might be asking yourself what is the difference between sin and a sinful nature. The sinful nature is your lifestyle, the sins you do repeatedly, where sin is just individual sins, the not repeating sins that occur less often. Also in the next verse it will talk about a punishment of hell as well.

**2 Peter 2:4-6** *"For if God spared not the angels that sinned, but cast them down to hell, and delivered them into chains of darkness, to be reserved unto judgment; And spared not the old world, but saved Noah the eighth person, a preacher of righteousness, bringing in the flood upon the world of the ungodly; And turning the cities of*

*Sodom and Gomorrah into ashes condemned them with an overthrow, making them an ensample unto those that after should live ungodly."* (King James) This verse explains that God will destroy the ungodly like he did in Noah's time and how he destroyed Sodom and Gomorrah and he didn't wait for them to die of natural causes, he ended their life because they were wicked.

What is the result of becoming a Christian and then not repenting of your sins after living as a Christian? This also is the scripture that totally destroys the "once saved, always saved" doctrine.

**Hebrews 10:26-31** *"If we deliberately keep on sinning after we have received the knowledge of the truth, no sacrifice for sins is left, but only a fearful expectation of judgment and of raging fire that will consume the enemies of God. Anyone who rejected the law of Moses died without mercy on the testimony of two or three witnesses. How much more severely do you think someone deserves to be punished who has trampled the Son of God underfoot, who has treated as an unholy thing the blood of the covenant that sanctified them, and who has insulted the Spirit of grace? For we know him who said, "It is mine to avenge; I will repay," and again, "The Lord will judge his people." It is a dreadful thing to fall into the hands of the living God"* (NIV)

This scripture has some good points we need to recognize. It is talking to people who have received the knowledge of the truth. It is also talking to those who have been sanctified because it says in **verse 29** *"to those who have been sanctified."* sanctified has to do with being recreated holy and that is done by the blood of Jesus.

Another point of the scripture is about the result of not repenting of yours sins after becoming a true Christian. The result is a *"fearful expectation of judgment and raging fire"* (NIV) that will devour you. So you will be consumed of judgment and hell, and it will terrify you. So this will be a sign to you that you are not saved, the fear of going to hell.

Finally, we are going to talk about the capital punishment of breaking the Mosaic Law or just the punishment of the worst sins. **Deuteronomy 21:22-23** *"And if a man have committed a sin worthy of death, and he be put to death, and thou hang him on a tree; his body shall not remain all night upon the tree, but thou shalt surely bury him the same day; for he that is hanged is accursed of God; that thou defile not thy land which Jehovah thy God giveth thee for an inheritance."* (American Standard Version) Back in the Old Testament times, being hung on a tree actually meant being crucified to a tree, and it also was God's curse or the capital punishment for breaking the law. In **Galatians 3:10-13**, the word "curse" of the law is being translated as "punishment" of the law And then goes on to say, *"Cursed is everyone that hangeth on a tree,"* (American Standard Version) which in the Greek basically means "under punishment" is everyone hung on a tree.

The scripture reads this way in **Galatians 3:10-13** *"For as many as are of the works of the law are under a curse: for it is written, Cursed is every one who continueth not in all things that are written in the book of the law, to do them. Now that no man is justified by the law before God, is evident: for, The righteous shall live by faith and the law is not of faith; but, He that doeth them shall live in them. Christ redeemed us from the curse of the law, having become a curse for us; for it is written, Cursed is every one that hangeth on a tree"* (American Standard Version) by becoming the "one on whom the punishment rests" for us; and the punishment fell on Jesus when he was crucified.

So let's recap. The Bible says there is no one righteous, and for all have sinned and fallen short of the glory of God and the law is there to make us conscious of our sin. We have also gone over the acts of the sinful nature. Finally, we have found out that the penalty of breaking God's law or more importantly the capital punishment for breaking God's law is to be hung on a tree, which means just to be crucified. Not all of God's laws had a penalty of being nailed to a tree just the worst sins. Some other punishment of sins was maybe to sacrifice a bull or another animal but when the sin was bad enough they had to crucify the sinner as a penalty for the offense.

## Notes

## Chapter 4

# Does God save us because we do good deeds or good works?

*B*efore we ask ourselves "Why did he save us?" we must first ask ourselves "What did he save us from?" The first thing he saved us from was a separated relationship from God, which he saved us from in order that we might become children of God (**Gal. 4:4-7**). The next thing he saved us from was the penalty of our sin and that was to be crucified to a tree. Lastly, he saved us from going to hell after we die?

Why did God choose to save us? Is it because I fed the poor? Is it because I invited people to my church? Is it because I read the Bible every day? Is it because I prayed to him? Is it because I thanked him for my food? Is it because I confessed my sins to another person? Absolutely not! God didn't decide to save us because we did these things, nor is our salvation linked to these things. The most important thing to God is to trust his promise about Jesus not to do good works to prove we believe. The book of **Romans 4:4** says *"Now to the one who works, wages are not credited as a gift but as an obligation. However, to the one who does not work but trusts God who justifies the ungodly, their faith is credited as righteousness"* (NIV) So basically, if you are trying to do good things in order to receive salvation or in order to stay saved, then it is no longer a gift but an obligation. What God wants is our trust in Christ's sacrifice versus doing good deeds. The Bible says in **Ephesians 2:8-10** *"For it is by grace you have been saved, through faith—and this is not from yourselves, it is the gift of God— not by works, so that no one can boast. For we are God's handiwork, created in Christ Jesus to do good works, which God prepared in advance for us to do"* (NIV)

So he did create us to do good works, but not to save us. If it wasn't because of our works that he saved us, then why did he save us? He saved us because he pitied us and loved us. In **Titus 3:4-5** *"But when the kindness and love of God our Savior appeared, he saved us, not because of righteous things we had done, but because of his mercy. He saved us through the washing of rebirth and renewal by the Holy Spirit"* (NIV) The word mercy has a synonym of pity; he pitied us. In **John 3:16** *"For God so loved the world that he gave his one and only Son, that whoever believes in him shall not perish but have eternal life."* (NIV) So this scripture says he saved us because he loved us (the world).

Another scripture that talks about why he saved us is **2 Timothy 1:9** *"He has saved us and called us to a holy life—not because of anything we have done but because of his own purpose and grace. This grace was given us in Christ Jesus before the beginning of time."* (NIV) So you see it was God's purpose to save us and it was by grace.

How many righteous acts were involved in saving us? Just one! **Romans 5:18** *"Consequently, just as one trespass resulted in condemnation for all people, so also one righteous act resulted in justification and life for all people."* (NIV) So from this verse, there was only one righteous act involved that brought justification, not two or three or anymore. Which means that none of our added good deeds save us which totally disagrees with what the book of James says and I reiterate this later in the book. James says in chapter 2 vs 14 *"What doth it profit, my brethren, though a man say he hath faith, and have not works? can faith save him?"* (King James) You can tell that James is implying that your faith can't save you without doing good deeds as well. But in **Romans 4:6** it says that we are given our righteousness or without our works, which means our righteousness or our salvation is given to us without our works. Also in **Romans 4:4** it says when we are working for our gift then it is no longer a gift but an obligation. So if you are doing good deeds to prove you believe then you really don't believe. You are trusting in yourself and your good deeds to save you and not trusting in the cross. I declare to you that it is only the death, burial, and resurrection that saves you, like **1 Corinthians 15:1-5** says and it is by faith, not deeds.

Did he save us by our obedience? It wasn't by our obedience. It was by his obedience. **Romans 5:19 "so also through the obedience of the one man the many will be made righteous."** *(NIV)* That one man is Jesus Christ, and that obedience is death on the cross.

# Notes

# Chapter 5

# What was the free gift?

*J*esus was the free gift given by God. (Meditate on that for a little while. It helped me to meditate about Jesus being the free gift.)

**John 3:16** *"For God so loved the world that he gave his one and only Son, that whoever believes in him shall not perish but have eternal life."* (NIV) God gave his Son. Once you realize that Jesus was the free gift, you'll realize your works have nothing to do with you salvation.

**Romans 5:15** *"But the gift is not like the trespass. For if the many died by the trespass of the one man, how much more did God's grace and the gift that came by the grace of the one man, Jesus Christ, overflow to the many"* (NIV)

　　Eternal life is free.

**Romans 6:23** *"For the wages of sin is death, but the gift of God is eternal life in Christ Jesus our Lord"* (NIV)

　　Salvation is free.

**Ephesians 2:8** *"For it is by grace you have been saved, through faith—and this is not from yourselves, it is the gift of God"* (NIV)

Finally, the Holy Spirit is a free gift.

**Acts 2:38** *"Peter replied, "Repent and be baptized, every one of you, in the name of Jesus Christ for the forgiveness of your sins. And you will receive the gift of the Holy Spirit.'"* (NIV)

- Jesus Christ was free.
- Eternal life is free.
- Salvation is free.
- The Holy Spirit was a free gift.

So you see none of these that has been given to us did we have to work for or do good deeds to receive. You may ask yourself, "Is being baptized a good deed?" No, because someone else is dunking or baptizing you; they are doing the work. You are allowing God to give you salvation at baptism. If you were fighting getting baptized you would be working, but you are allowing someone to baptize you or give you the gift of salvation.

## Notes

## Chapter 6

# How do I receive the free gift?

Let me ask you a question, "When someone gives you a birthday gift, don't you have to reach out and take it from their hands and tear it open?" Does that mean you are working to get that birthday gift because you reached out to take it from his hands and tore it open? No. It's the same way with salvation. Salvation has stipulations on how to receive the gift. How do we take the gift from God?

The following verses tell us how to receive the gift of the Holy Spirit:

**Galatians 3:2-6** *"I would like to learn just one thing from you: Did you receive the Spirit by the works of the law, or by believing what you heard? Are you so foolish? After beginning by means of the Spirit, are you now trying to finish by means of the flesh? Have you experienced so much in vain—if it really was in vain? So again I ask, does God give you his Spirit and work miracles among you by the works of the law, or by your believing what you heard? So also Abraham "believed God, and it was credited to him as righteousness." (NIV)*

You may ask yourself "What is the message I need to have heard to know what to believe?"

**Ephesians 1:13-14** *"And you also were included in Christ when you heard the message of truth, the gospel of your salvation. When you believed, you were marked in him with a seal, the promised Holy Spirit, who is a deposit guaranteeing our inheritance until the redemption of those who are God's possession—to the praise of his glory." (NIV)* So this verse also tells us we receive the Holy Spirit by believing the gospel of our salvation. But even before believing comes hearing the gospel. **Romans 10:17** says, *"Consequently, faith comes from hearing the message, and the message is heard through the word about Christ."* (NIV)

You might be asking yourself, "What is the message or the gospel of our salvation?" Let's take a look at **1 Corinthians 15:1-8**

*"Now, brothers and sisters, I want to remind you of the gospel I preached to you, which you received and on which you have taken your stand. By this gospel you are saved, if you hold firmly to the word I preached to you. Otherwise, you have believed in vain." (NIV)* In **verse 3**, *"For what I received I passed on to you as of first importance: that Christ died for our sins according to the Scriptures, that he was buried, that he was raised on the third day according to the Scriptures, and that he appeared to Cephas, and then to the Twelve. After that, he appeared to more than five hundred of the brothers and sisters at the same time, most of whom are still living, though some have fallen asleep. Then he appeared to James, then to all the apostles, and last of all he appeared to me also, as to one abnormally born." (NIV)*

That is the gospel; that he died for our sins, and that he was buried and that he was raised again on the third day. Another scripture that talks about what we need to believe is **Roman 3:25** *"Whom God hath set forth to be a propitiation through faith in his blood, to declare his righteousness for the remission of sins that are past, through the forbearance of God."* (King James)

The word propitiation in the original Greek means he is the place the sinner unloads his sin and he is also the thing that pays the penalty. Also, the word blood in this scripture is translated as "the type of death that occurred, like a gruesome death" —not the blood flowing through his veins, but his death or murder. So we have to have faith in his "gruesome death" for our sins. It is also not just any type of death either. It is death on a cross. So basically **Romans 3:25** means God presented Jesus as a sacrifice that would pay the penalty of our sins through faith in his gruesome death for our sins.

In **1 Peter 2:24**, it says, *"He himself bore our sins in his body on the cross, so that we might die to sins and live for righteousness; "by his wounds you have been healed."* (NIV) The words "bore our sins" mean to carry the load or carry the punishment of our sin. So the punishment occurred while on the tree, not in hell or in the grave.

In **Hebrews 10:14**, it says, *"For by one sacrifice he has made perfect forever those who are being made holy."* (NIV) It was his one sacrifice that made us perfect.

In **Hebrews 10:10**, it says. *"And by that will, we have been made holy through the sacrifice of the body of Jesus Christ once for all."* (NIV) So it was his physical body that was sacrificed to make us holy.

In **Colossians 1:22**, it says, *"But now he has reconciled you by Christ's physical body through death to present you holy in his sight, without blemish and free from accusation."* (NIV) Another thing is he didn't pay the penalty for our sins in hell either. The previous two scriptures testify to that.

Finally, the last scripture that I'm going to share about the fact that it was a physical body and death was in **Hebrews 2:14** *"Since the children have flesh and blood, he too shared in their humanity so that by his death he might break the power of him who holds the power of death—that is, the devil"* (NIV) (death being spiritually separated from God, which means you are not forgiven)—In **verse 17**, *"For this reason he had to be made like them, fully human in every way, in order that he might become a merciful and faithful high priest in service to God, and that he might make atonement for the sins of the people."(NIV)* The reason he had to be made like a human was in order pay the penalty for the sins of a human, you had to be human; it was like an even trade—his death on the cross for your penalty of death on a cross. He also was made human because he had to be tempted in every way as we are and be without sin and because he was tempted he would also then be more merciful.

Just a couple of interesting bits of information from scripture that says when the penalty was paid was in **Matthew 27:50-51** *"And when Jesus had cried out again in a loud voice, he gave up his spirit.*

*At that moment the curtain of the temple was torn in two from top to bottom. The earth shook, the rocks split."* (NIV) In the temple, the curtain is what separated the Holy Place from the Most Holy Place; it is what separated us from our relationship with God. In **Hebrews 10:19-20**, it says, *"Therefore, brothers and sisters, since we have confidence to enter the Most Holy Place by the blood of Jesus, by a new and living way opened for us through the curtain, that is, his body."* (NIV) So once the curtain is torn, we can enter the Most Holy Place and have a relationship with God, and the way the curtain is torn is through the death of Jesus's body on the cross.

What else do we need to believe? **Romans 10:8-9** *"But what does it say? "The word is near you; it is in your mouth and in your heart," that is, the message concerning faith that we proclaim: If you declare with your mouth, "Jesus is Lord," and believe in your heart that God raised him from the dead, you will be saved."* (NIV) So we've got to believe that God raised him from the dead.

Let's talk about what this believing from the heart actually means. The word heart is actually translated to mean intellectual mind or the inmost mind" It also could be translated as the part of the mind that does the grasping and understanding. This implies that you should understand and believe what your intellect is telling you. So believing from the heart means believing from the intellectual mind or believing with comprehension from your intelligence. So you got understand and believe that God raised Jesus from the dead from your inmost intelligence.

Back to the scripture in **1 Corinthians 15:2**, it says, *"By this gospel you are saved, if you hold firmly to the word I preached to you. Otherwise, you have believed in vain."* (NIV) Hold firmly in the Greek originally meant to grasp intellectually which also implies that you grasp the gospel or the death burial and resurrection.

Another scripture that implies that you should have understanding is **Hebrews 9:14** *"How much more, then, will the blood of Christ, who through the eternal Spirit offered himself unblemished to God, cleanse our consciences from acts that lead to death, so that we may serve the living God!"* (NIV) Why would the blood of Jesus cleanse our conscience because we understand that the penalty has been paid for and we will no longer feel guilty for our sins? It says this in **Hebrews 10:1** *"The law is only a shadow of the good things that are coming—not the realities themselves. For this reason it can never, by the same sacrifices repeated endlessly year after year, make perfect those who draw near to worship."* (NIV) In **verse 2**, *"Otherwise, would they not have stopped being offered? For the worshipers would have been cleansed once for all, and would no longer have felt guilty for their sins."* (NIV)

So if you comprehend the message of the cross and are saved, you will no longer feel guilty for your sins. But if you don't grasp that a penalty has been paid for, you will still feel guilty. What type of guilt will you feel? You might feel an impending doom is awaiting you. You also might feel like God hates you and the wrath of God is waiting for you. If you feel these things, you should take heed that you might not be saved. Now if you deliberately start sinning and are no longer repenting of your sins, you are going to feel guilty because you are going to lose your salvation. **Hebrews 10:26-27** *"If we deliberately keep on sinning after we have received the knowledge of the truth, no sacrifice for sins is left, but only a fearful expectation of judgment and of raging fire that will consume the enemies of God."* (NIV) But the main point I was trying to get at is you must understand the message of the cross in order to be saved by faith.

## Notes

## Chapter 7

# What is the process of one becoming a true Christian?

We've already talked about the first step and that is belief or faith in the gospel, the death, the burial, and the resurrection of Jesus Christ.

**1 Corinthians 15:1-7**

What is the second step in becoming a true Christian?

**Acts 2:38**

Repentance is the second step. You see Jesus didn't die for the sins that we won't repent of.

**Hebrews 10:26**

Let us take a look at some scriptures about repentance. The first and second scriptures tell us that repentance precedes salvation. **Acts 2:38** *"Peter replied, "Repent and be baptized, every one of you, in the name of Jesus Christ for the forgiveness of your sins. And you will receive the gift of the Holy Spirit."* (NIV) The second scripture is **2 Corinthians 7:10** *"Godly sorrow brings repentance that leads* *to salvation and leaves no regret, but worldly sorrow brings death."* (NIV) So these two verses tell us that we need to repent or turn from our sins in order to be saved.

Now let's look deeper at this description of repentance. Back to **2 Corinthians 7:10-11** *"Godly sorrow brings repentance that leads to salvation and leaves no regret, but worldly sorrow brings death. See what this godly sorrow has produced in you: what earnestness, what eagerness to clear yourselves, what indignation, what alarm, what longing, what concern, what readiness to see justice done."* (NIV) Another thing that should happen if you have repented of your sin is you should feel brokenness especially if you have sinned a lot. In **Luke 7:36-47** there was a sinful woman and she had cried probably about the sinful life she had lived and she loved Jesus more than the Pharisee in the story. Another example of brokenness is in **Psalm 51** and it is an excellent example of brokenness and repentance. It is after David had been confronted about his sin with Bathsheba.

Here is what it says in **Psalm 51:1-17**

*"Have mercy upon me, O God, according to thy lovingkindness: according unto the multitude of thy tender mercies blot out my transgressions.*
*Wash me throughly from mine iniquity, and cleanse me from my sin.*
*For I acknowledge my transgressions: and my sin is ever before me.*
*Against thee, thee only, have I sinned, and done this evil in thy sight: that thou mightest be justified when thou speakest, and be clear when thou judgest.*
*Behold, I was shapen in iniquity; and in sin did my mother conceive me.*
*Behold, thou desirest truth in the inward parts: and in the hidden part thou shalt make me to know wisdom.*

*Purge me with hyssop, and I shall be clean: wash me, and I shall be whiter than snow.*
*Make me to hear joy and gladness; that the bones which thou hast broken may rejoice.*
*Hide thy face from my sins, and blot out all mine iniquities.*
*Create in me a clean heart, O God; and renew a right spirit within me.*
*Cast me not away from thy presence; and take not thy holy spirit from me.*
*Restore unto me the joy of thy salvation; and uphold me with thy free spirit.*
*Then will I teach transgressors thy ways; and sinners shall be converted unto thee.*
*Deliver me from bloodguiltiness, O God, thou God of my salvation: and my tongue shall sing aloud of thy righteousness.*
*O Lord, open thou my lips; and my mouth shall shew forth thy praise.*
*For thou desirest not sacrifice; else would I give it: thou delightest not in burnt offering.*
*The sacrifices of God are a broken spirit: a broken and a contrite heart, O God, thou wilt not despise."*
*(King James)*

Here is another example of repentance in the Bible:
Zacchaeus, the Tax Collector

> **Luke 19:1-8** *"And Jesus entered and passed through Jericho.*
> *And, behold, there was a man named Zacchaeus, which was the chief among the publicans, and he was rich.*
> *And he sought to see Jesus who he was; and could not for the press, because he was little of stature.*
> *And he ran before, and climbed up into a sycomore tree to see him: for he was to pass that way.*
> *And when Jesus came to the place, he looked up, and saw him, and said unto him, Zacchaeus, make haste, and come down; for to day I must abide at thy house.*
> *And he made haste, and came down, and received him joyfully.*

*And when they saw it, they all murmured, saying, That he was gone to be guest with a man that is a sinner.*
*And Zacchaeus stood, and said unto the Lord: Behold, Lord, the half of my goods I give to the poor; and if I have taken anything from any man by false accusation, I restore him fourfold." (King James)*

So you see Zacchaeus had a repentant heart that was eager to change, and he was earnest and eager to clear himself.

What is the last step in becoming a true Christian? I reiterate these three verses before I go on to the last step. **John 12:47-48** *"If anyone hears my words but does not keep them, I do not judge that person. For I did not come to judge the world, but to save the world. There is a judge for the one who rejects me and does not accept my words; the very words I have spoken will condemn them at the last day."* (NIV) The next verse is **John 4:23-24** *"Yet a time is coming and has now come when the true worshipers will worship the Father in the Spirit and in truth, for they are the kind of worshipers the Father seeks. God is spirit, and his worshipers must worship in the Spirit and in truth."* (NIV) The reason I share these verses is because we have to realize we are going to be judged based on what the truth is not what our minister told us unless it was the truth. In **1 Kings 13:7-25** talks clearly about how God treats individuals who listen to people who claim to be prophets versus listening to what God actually taught. Basically, what happened was a man listened to someone who claimed to be a prophet but was lying to him and God had already told him to do something else and because he listened to the false prophet God sent a lion to come and kill the man for listening to the false prophet instead of God. So we always got to know what God says and obey him over false prophets. Anyone can be a false prophet even your own minister, that's why the challenge is to study out the scriptures on your own. In **Acts 17:11** it says *"Now the Berean Jews were of more noble character than those in Thessalonica, for they received the message with great eagerness and examined the Scriptures every day to see if what Paul said was true."* (NIV) The bible says they were noble because they tested the Apostle Paul's words and compared his words with other scriptures.

Now he was an apostle and you think it was ok to just trust him because he was an apostle but God says no you are noble if you examine other scriptures just to make sure it is in line with the truth. As you read further in Chapter 13 that is exactly what I do when I talk about the book of James. I compare all the scriptures about grace and compare to what James is implying in his teaching. As you should do the same, read closely to what James is saying don't twist it to mean something it is not saying. Also one other thing I want to make a note of is that if you are reading this book you need to be a Berean and study out the scriptures on your own, and realize also I may not be right about James because I see through the eyes of someone who has ADHD which makes it harder to discern the truth, but I may be right, as my health improves I will see whether James teaching is really from God or not. But I very confident about everything else in this book. The three things that are questionable is the book is the book of James truly God's word and whether or not the mentally disabled are saved by default because they can't understand, and lastly about confessing your sins to stay forgiven, which I go into more detail later on in this book. But just keep reading I do explain from my point of view what I think these topics are really saying.

Finally, The last step in becoming a Christian is covered in the rest of the chapter.

**Mark 16:16**: *"Whoever believes and is baptized will be saved,"* (NIV) Baptized in the original Greek means to submerse.

**John 3:3-5** *"Jesus replied, "Very truly I tell you, no one can see the kingdom of God unless they are born again. "How can someone be born when they are old?" Nicodemus asked. "Surely they cannot enter a second time into their mother's womb to be born!" Jesus answered, "Very truly I tell you, no one can enter the kingdom of God unless they are born of water and the Spirit."* (NIV) The water is referring to baptism.

**Acts 22:16** *"And now what are you waiting for? Get up, be baptized, and wash your sins away, calling on his name."* (NIV) So you see we are washing our sins away at baptism. You may ask how are we washing our sins away. We have already found out that it is Jesus's death that has paid the penalty. Well, the way we are washing them away is that our sins are being transferred from our body and being placed onto Jesus's body at baptism. It's kind of like in the Old Testament sacrifices when the priest laid hands on the animal sacrifice to kill the animal, the sins were being transferred to the animal at the laying on of the hands and then it was sacrificed.

What role does baptism actually play? In **1 Peter 3:21** *"And this water symbolizes baptism that now saves you also—not the removal of dirt from the body but the pledge of a clear conscience toward God. It saves you by the resurrection of Jesus Christ."* (NIV) (The pledge of a good conscience toward God, I believe, is the promise of a cleansed conscience toward God through Jesus interceding for us and washing our guilty conscience.) In **Verse 21 it says** *"It saves you by the resurrection of Jesus Christ."* (NIV) How does the resurrection save you? Basically, it saves you because in order for a high priest to intercede for you he had to be alive to bring to the altar the sacrifice to pay your penalty. So Jesus has to be alive in order to bring his sacrifice to the altar of God. Let's look at **Hebrews 7:23-25** *"Now there have been many of those priests, since death prevented them from continuing in office; but because Jesus lives forever, he has a permanent priesthood. Therefore he is able to save completely those who come to God through him, because he always lives to intercede for them."* (NIV)

**Romans 6:3-5** *"Or don't you know that all of us who were baptized into Christ Jesus were baptized into his death? We were therefore buried with him through baptism into death in order that, just as Christ was raised from the dead through the glory of the Father, we too may live a new life. For if we have been united with him in a death like his, we will certainly also be united with him in a resurrection like his."* (NIV) This scripture goes on to say that we are baptized into his death, which means we are placed into his death, and that is how we actually get the covering for our sins. It also says that we have to be united with him at baptism in order to be united with him at the resurrection. In **Galatians 3:26-27** *"So in Christ Jesus you are all children of God through faith, for all of you who were baptized into Christ have clothed yourselves with Christ."* (NIV) So basically, it is saying we need to be baptized in order to be clothed with Christ. What does it mean to be clothed with Christ? It means his death covers ours sins, and that he died for us, and that we had enough faith in Christ to be baptized.

In **Matthew 28:18-20** it says that we are to be baptized by the name of the Father, the Son, and the Holy Spirit. Which I believe means being baptized by the power and authority of the Father, Son, and the Holy Spirit. It is their authority that allows anyone to be baptized into Christ. I also know that I am being baptized into the name of Jesus for salvation, and it is actually that name that saves us. In **Acts 4:12**, *"Salvation is found in no one else, for there is no other name under heaven given to mankind by which we must be saved."* (NIV) Another thing to think about is in **Romans 8:1** *"Therefore, there is now no condemnation for those who are in Christ Jesus."* (NIV) How do we get into Christ Jesus but to be baptized into him, like **Galatians 3:26-27** says?

Another thought people say, "What about the thief on the cross? He wasn't baptized." **Matthew 9:6** *"But I want you to know that the Son of Man has authority on earth to forgive sins."* (NIV) Jesus had the authority while on this earth to forgive sins, and he did that while he was on this earth.

Something else to think about was being baptized is actually taking part in the death, burial, and resurrection, and the thief on the cross couldn't be baptized into Jesus death because Jesus had not died yet. God didn't command people did get baptized into Jesus until he had been crucified and buried and resurrected. In **Acts 2:38** that is when people started getting baptized into Christ, which was after Jesus died and was buried and resurrected.

Another thing was how can the Holy Spirit be a gift if we are baptized. It says in **Acts 2:38** *"Peter replied, "Repent and be baptized, every one of you, in the name of Jesus Christ for the forgiveness of your sins. And you will receive the gift of the Holy Spirit."*

(NIV) So you see even the Bible says that the Holy Spirit is still a gift after repenting and being baptized. Also being baptized isn't a good deed it's an act of faith because you are publicly confessing your faith at baptism.

The last part of conversion or becoming a saved individual is calling on the name of the Lord or confessing Jesus is Lord. The word says in **Romans 10:8-9** *"But what does it say? "The word is near you; it is in your mouth and in your heart," that is, the message concerning faith that we proclaim: If you declare with your mouth, "Jesus is Lord," and believe in your heart that God raised him from the dead, you will be saved."* (NIV)

**Romans 10:13** *"Everyone who calls on the name of the Lord will be saved."* (NIV)

When do we call on the name of the Lord? At baptism.

**Acts 8:36-38** (*The Ethiopian Eunuch*) (NIV) As your reading this, read also the footnote in the bible. It talks about him confessing Jesus as the Son of The Most High. So you see that the eunuch confessed that Jesus is the Son of God at baptism.

**Acts 22:16** Saul (*Paul's baptism*). *"And now what are you waiting for? Get up, be baptized and wash your sins away, calling on his name."* (NIV)

To sum it all up, the true way to be saved is to believe that Jesus died for our sins, that he was buried, and that he was raised from the dead. We must then repent and turn from our sins, and then we must confess Jesus is Lord and be baptized by the Authority of the name of the Father, the Son, and the Holy Spirit.

## Notes

# Chapter 8

# What is the proof of my salvation?

**1 Peter 1:8-9** *"Though you have not seen him, you love him; and even though you do not see him now, you believe in him and are filled with an inexpressible and glorious joy, for you are receiving the end result of your faith, the salvation of your souls." (NIV)*

This scripture tells us that if we believe in him, we will have an inexpressible and glorious joy, and this will be a sign that we are receiving the goal of our faith, the salvation of our souls. One thing to realize is that the joy we have is one of the fruits of the Spirit, but also to realize that this joy will be incredible and it must be glorious, and words won't be able to describe how it will feel.

Another scripture that talks about the proof that will be in our life if we are saved and have God's Holy Spirit is **Galatians 5:22-23** *"But the fruit of the Spirit is love, joy, peace, forbearance, kindness, goodness, faithfulness, gentleness and self-control. Against such things there is no law."* (NIV)

One of the descriptions that talks about the peace we will have is **Philippians 4:7** *"And the peace of God, which transcends all understanding, will guard your hearts and your minds in Christ Jesus."* (NIV) God's peace that he gives us transcends all understanding and that peace will be pretty amazing.

Finally, we will have cleansed conscience. The blood of Jesus will wash or cleanse our guilty conscience. Just read the book of **Hebrews** and it will talk about that in **Chapters 9-10**. Specifically in **Hebrews 9:14** it says he cleanses our conscience, in order that we are able to serve him. We can't serve him if we feel guilty all the time. Also in **Hebrews 10:2** it says that once we are cleansed of our sins we will no longer feel guilty. So just read those two chapters to get a better idea.

This scripture tells us how we know we are saved just by looking at our lifestyle. **1 John 2:6 "Whoever claims to live in him must live as Jesus did."** (NIV) That doesn't mean that the good deeds we do like Jesus did save us. Only faith, repentance, baptism, and confessing Jesus is Lord saves us, but it is truly the faith that saves us at baptism. So what does this scripture tell us: that if we are walking like Jesus then we really do live in him and are saved? Walking like Jesus is just a testimonial of our faith; it is one proof that we are believers. In **Romans 1:5**, it says, *"Through him we received grace and apostleship to call all the Gentiles to the obedience that comes from faith for his name's sake"* (NIV) We will have obedience if we truly have faith; obedience is a proof of our faith. As we live obedient lives that will remind us every day that we are believers of Christ.

So let's recap. The first proof of our salvation is we will have a joy that is incredible, second we will have a peace that is beyond our understanding, third our conscience will be cleansed so that we no longer feel guilty, next we see that our lives will live like Jesus did, and lastly we will be obedient to Christ.

# Notes

# Chapter 9

# What is the proof that I might not be saved?

§§

*F*irst off, a feeling that we won't have when we aren't saved is joy that we can't express what it's like in our heart and we won't have peace that passes comprehension in our hearts. It also means is our hearts won't feel refreshed in our relationship with God or won't feel grateful toward God, we will feel guilty and afraid. In **Acts 3:19**, *"Repent, then, and turn to God, so that your sins may be wiped out, that times of refreshing may come from the Lord,"* (NIV) If we are still living in sin or following the sinful nature, then we aren't saved. **Galatians 5:24** *"Those who belong to Christ Jesus have crucified the flesh with its passions and desires."* (NIV) Also in **1 John 3:9-10** *"No one who is born of God will continue to sin, because God's seed remains in them; they cannot go on sinning, because they have been born of God."* (NIV) That doesn't mean we won't sin, it just means we won't live following after our sinful nature. **Verse 10** *"This is how we know who the children of God are and who the children of the devil are: Anyone who does not do what is right is not God's child, nor is anyone who does not love their brother and sister."* (NIV) So it is clear that you are not saved if aren't doing the right things, or if you haven't put to death the fleshly nature.

Another thing, you aren't saved if you haven't repented of your sins and been baptized with faith that Jesus died for your sins and called on the name of the Lord.

**1 John 2:15-17** *"Do not love the world or anything in the world. If anyone loves the world, love for the Father is not in them. For everything in the world—the lust of the flesh, the lust of the eyes, and the pride of life—comes not from the Father but from the world. The world and its desires pass away, but whoever does the will of God lives forever."* (NIV) I reiterate that the will of God is to believe in the name of God's One and Only Son. **John 6:28-29** *"Then they asked him, "What must we do to do the works God requires?" Jesus answered, "The work of God is this: to believe in the one he has sent.'"* (NIV)

A couple other scriptures that talk about who isn't saved is:

**1 John 2:9** *"Anyone who claims to be in the light but hates a brother or sister is still in the darkness." (NIV)* The scripture is referring to our brothers and sisters in Christ. But I also know that God doesn't want us to hate anyone else either. If we hate anyone that may be a sign that we aren't saved because we usually hate people we haven't forgiven for something. What scripture talks about this? **Matthew 6:14-15** *"For if you forgive other people when they sin against you, your heavenly Father will also forgive you. But if you do not forgive others their sins, your Father will not forgive your sins."* (NIV)

What kind of things will God do to try and get your attention to help you see that you're not saved?
He will allow you to fear death or just be terrified of him and think he is an angry God. Sometimes he might scare you in your circumstances whenever you sin. He will allow you to feel guilty when you sin, and you won't have a cleansed conscience. I personally have felt these things. I've even felt like God is going to put me to death at times. One scripture that talks about fear of dying is **Hebrews 2:14-15** *"Since the children have flesh and blood, he too shared in their humanity so that by his death he might break the*

*power of him who holds the power of death—that is, the devil— and free those who all their lives were held in slavery by their fear of death."* (NIV) So you see God will free you from your fear of death if you are saved.

In **Romans 8:15**, it says, *"The Spirit you received does not make you slaves, so that you live in fear again; rather, the Spirit you received brought about your adoption to sonship. And by him we cry, "Abba, Father."* (NIV) This verse tells us that if we are fearing him then we don't have God's Spirit because in the rest of the verse it says that we will cry out dad" (NIV) by his Spirit, which is like crying daddy; it is a term of endearment. You can tell if you fear him or if you love him like he is your daddy.

Another scripture on fear is **1 John 4:16-18** *"And so we know and rely on the love God has for us.*
*God is love. Whoever lives in love lives in God, and God in them. This is how love is made complete among us so that we will have confidence on the day of judgment: In this world we are like Jesus. There is no fear in love. But perfect love drives out fear, because fear has to do with punishment. The one who fears is not made perfect in love."* (NIV) Fear is an emotion that God has given us to motivate us to seek him in order to be saved. Fear is not a lie from Satan. We may very well not be saved if we fear dying, because perfect love drives out fear. If we struggle with fear, a few things need to occur. We need to study out the love of God, which is throughout the Old Testament, and the cross of Jesus. Another thing to study out is **Nehemiah 9**. In this chapter, it talks about all the sin the Israelites were getting into, and it was a lot of sin and how after all the sin they had committed, God was still willing to forgive them as soon as they repented and called back on the Lord. It is a perfect example of how we can lose our forgiveness and get it right back as soon as we repent and call back on the Lord. Also read the book of Judges. There are number of examples of people coming back to God, after falling away, just as as soon as they repent.

The one scripture that brings fear into people's hearts but is misinterpreted by many is in **Hebrews 6:4-6** *"It is impossible for those* *who have once been enlightened, who have tasted the heavenly gift, who have shared in the Holy Spirit, who have tasted the goodness of the word of God and the powers of the coming age and who have fallen away, to be brought back to repentance. To their loss they are crucifying the Son of God all over again and subjecting him to public disgrace"* (NIV) The reason people are afraid when they read this is because they are afraid they won't be able to come back to God if they leave him. But really what it is saying is that while you are in a state of non-repentance and are subjecting him to public to grace you can't be saved while you are not repenting, so as long as you repent you can come back to him you can be saved. Just read the story of the prodigal son, he left his father and took the inheritance and squandered it with wild living and he decided to come back to his father and was received back with open arms and the father even threw a party to celebrate his return. But mainly, the cross should cause us to not fear God because it is God's ultimate message of love. Actually, if we truly believe in the cross we will not fear dying. Lastly, one final proof that we aren't saved is we will still feel guilty and won't feel cleansed of our sins. In **Hebrews 10:2** *"For the worshipers would have been cleansed once for all, and would no longer have felt guilty for their sins."* (NIV) Cleansed means washed, and it implies that when we are cleansed of our sins, we will no longer feel guilty. So if we feel guilty, it is telling us that either we haven't received forgiveness or we just need to repent of our sin. Our conscience is guiding us, letting us know that we are still guilty and not forgiven or in need of repentance. We need to listen to our conscience. **Hebrews 9:14** says that we can't serve God without a cleansed conscience. One of the whole purposes of having a cleansed conscience is so we can serve God without fear or guilt, so we can feel free and close to our Father.

So let's go over again those things that will tell us we aren't saved yet. We won't have the joy of our salvation yet, we won't feel refreshed in our relationship with God, we will still be living after our sinful nature, we won't always try and do the right thing, we will love the world, next we might have not forgiven everyone in our life, we will be afraid of God, and lastly we will feel guilty and our conscience will not be cleansed. Finally, we have the proof that if we have repented, been baptized, and called on the name of the Lord and had faith in the death, burial, and resurrection, that would be the final proof we aren't saved yet.

## Notes

**Chapter 10**

# Can I still be saved when I have mental illness and can't understand what I am reading?

ॐ

*A*s I think about the title of this chapter I want to tell myself that God wouldn't punish those that are mentally handicapped and can't understand the Bible. I also want to believe that there is a certain point where someone can absolutely do nothing to help themselves get better from mental disease maybe they have no thinking capability at all, so that they can't get better on their own. Because of my mental disability it is hard to grasp how he feels about the mentally handicapped. So let's hope and pray that God will not punish those people and I'm pretty sure he won't. There is a couple of verses that confirm that and make me think that those that are mentally disabled are already saved is in the scripture is **Matthew 19:14** and **Luke 18:16** and it says that the children and those like children belong to God's Kingdom. I do believe that if we do have the capability to get better, we should do everything we possibly can because of what other scriptures say about God like in **Luke 12:47-49** *"The servant who knows the master's will and does not get ready or does not do what the master wants will be beaten with many blows. But the one who does not know and does things deserving punishment will be beaten with few blows. From everyone who has been given much, much will be demanded; and from the* *one who has been entrusted with much, much more will be asked."* (NIV) I do know one thing just because you are mentally handicapped doesn't mean you shouldn't try and get better, because we are still going to be judged based on what we are capable of doing, not what we cannot possibly do. It also says in **Luke 13:24** that basically we need to do everything possible we can to be saved.

I speak as someone who went from hardly any processing capability at all, but I had enough capability to read different books to figure out how to be healed. But, I do want to give you something else to think about. I know at times I have felt fear and guilt and haven't had a cleansed conscience and those were reminders of how God was still trying to tell me that I wasn't saved yet. Those things (the fear, guilt, and uncleansed conscience) were like him letting my conscience know that I was not saved by faith because my illness prevented my faith. I also think he could just be teaching me I need to be more obedient to him, I don't know.

But back to the end of the previous chapter. God might send frightening events in your life in order to give you a wake-up call. There also might be events that just scare us and get us to think about death. These signs will tell you whether you fear death, and that will tell you whether or not you are saved, along with a guilty conscience and little nudges or prodding to find out more about salvation, because if they are causing you fear, then fear is a sign that there is an impending punishment waiting. The Bible says in 1 John that *"fear has to do with punishment"* (NIV) **(1 John 4:18)**.

Something else to think about, we are justified by faith, which means we are made right with God by believing what our inmost mind tells us about God raising Jesus from the dead and mentally holding onto his death for our sins. If we don't have a mentally sharp mind and can't understand that, how can we believe it? And the Bible does talk a lot about us being saved through faith which includes understanding and comprehending the message. Let me give you an example. If someone reads to you something in a foreign language and then asks if you believe it, you can't make that decision to believe it if you don't understand what he is saying. Attention-deficit disorder can cause you to not be able to comprehend, grasp, or even understand what you are reading. When you do have different mental disabilities and your brain doesn't work and you can't comprehend what you are reading it's like a mentally normal person reading a sentence with all kinds of words that they don't know what they mean because they have never heard of those words before, but with a mentally disabled person they don't even know what the words mean even after looking them up in a dictionary. So basically you can't grasp that Jesus has been raised from the dead or that he has paid the penalty of your sin, so the fear and guilt remains on our conscience. One of the purposes of believing that Jesus died for our sins is so we can have a cleansed conscience. That means that our guilty feeling gets washed away, which means it is taken from us. **Hebrews 9:14** *"How much more, then, will the blood of Christ, who through the eternal Spirit offered himself unblemished to God, cleanse our consciences from acts that lead to death, so that we may serve the living God!"* (NIV) So you see that we can't serve God if we don't have a cleansed conscience. When we don't understand the concept or teaching of the cross, then his blood or death will not cleanse our conscience.

How do we make sure we can get this cleansed conscience? We must make sure our mental health is in tip-top shape.

**1 Corinthians 3:16-17** *"Don't you know that you yourselves are God's temple and that God's Spirit dwells in your midst? If anyone destroys God's temple, God will destroy that person; for God's temple is sacred, and you together are that temple."* (NIV)

How do we destroy that temple but by putting toxins in our body that destroy our mental health and understanding capability. Now I'm not saying it's completely your fault if you have your mental problems. But if as an adult you don't try to get healed, then it is your fault for not trying to get better. In **Philippians 2:12** it says, *"continue to work out your salvation with fear and trembling."* (NIV) So if we aren't saved by faith because of our health problems, then we need to get healed and do what **Philippians 2:12** says.

I'll give you a little hint: heavy metal poisoning causes many mental disabilities. What you can do is go to the Internet search engine and type in World Health Organizations statements on

Mercury poisoning. Also type in Center for disease control and mercury poisoning.) How do we get this poisoning? We get it from our silver-colored or dark-colored amalgam dental fillings and other flu and childhood vaccinations. I am not sure if braces or gold-colored teeth cause any problems, but it would be worth your time to get on the internet and find out. I remember two times I got dental fillings, one as a child and one time as an adult, that within thirty minutes of getting the dental fillings I got a worse case of attention-deficit disorder, which put a stop on me understanding and having faith in the gospel because I couldn't grasp it. It took me ten years of reading the bible and studying salvation to realize that the reason I couldn't have faith and understanding was because I had attention and comprehension problems, and I got this from my amalgam dental fillings. Did you know that the silver-colored dental fillings contain 50 percent mercury, and mercury is the second most toxic metal on the planet next to uranium? It is known to scientists that mercury and other toxic heavy metals affect the nervous system and brain functions. Each dental filling releases somewhere around 15 mcgs of mercury vapor into your body each day which can damage the brain cells.

We also get these toxins from eating farm-raised fish, catfish, salmon, tuna, etc. I personally believe that drinking out of aluminum cans can cause attention span problems because of the aluminum in the cans. I remember that the first time I drank out of a can of soda my attention span got worse. I also remember it happening after I had been detoxifying for a while, and when I had a can of soda, it got worse again. Do the research and find out that depression, attention-deficit disorder, schizophrenia, and bipolar and other mental disabilities come from these dental fillings and other heavy metals. So, I am urging you, you've got to get these fillings removed and go to a holistic dentist who is specially trained in removing these type of fillings or you could have worse health problems.

You can also get heavy metals poisoning from drinking water that hasn't been purified enough and that could have caused many people problems as well. After getting your fillings removed and to get better from this type of poisoning you need to get on some sort of detox program. Two programs that is able to remove these heavy metals are either Zeolite or DMSA. These two products are health supplements that attract themselves to the toxic metals and the liver pulls these supplements out of the body along with the metal attached with it. This is known as chelation therapy. With Zeolite it could take a number of months. I could tell it was helping me. But with DMSA therapy, it took me the longest. At least that has been my experience, but it may vary by individual. What I have read is the quickest way to remove these toxins is through eating ¼ cup of cilantro every day and then drinking plenty of fluids following that. It is also important to take crack-celled chlorella before eating the cilantro. Also, with eating cilantro, I have read that you should blend it up or use a supplement of concentrated cilantro. I personally could not tell any difference from eating the cilantro. I'm not sure which way is the quickest. I kind of think just drinking 20 to 30 grams of crack-celled chlorella powder in water by itself will do good too (before bedtime is the best.) But I do know you can tell which way works the best after testing each one and comparing with the improvement you feel.

Also another thing I have noticed that has helped was to make sure I take either the DMSA or the Zeolite right before I have a bowel movement. You should also drink plenty of water with these supplements because the water carries the supplement around the bloodstream to collect and flush out the unwanted heavy metals. It seems to work better that way. But it should be at 30 minutes to an hour before your bowel movement so that you can get the Chlorella or the Zeolite around in your system better and have a way to release the toxins when you got to the bathroom. Two other important things is you shouldn't be taking all these at the same time and you should also supplement with minerals on your off days or it could cause you problems like it did me. The minerals are needed especially if you are drinking a lot of water because as you are drinking all this water you are flushing out important minerals that the body needs.

Just to let you know, I am not a doctor and this information on diseases and treating them was all obtained by doing personal research and it does not guarantee a cure for your disease and is only for educational purposes. You really should find a Holistic Doctor or a naturopath doctor to help with your disease. But do the research, get on the internet, read all the testimonies, and then make some decisions. There are probably some other reasons for attention span problems, and the other mental disabilities, for example some mineral and vitamin deficiency can cause certain problems too, even Magnesium deficiency can cause anxiety, obsessive compulsive disorder, depression, attention, and comprehension problems. The best way for to absorb Magnesium is to soak in Epsom salt for about 30 minutes a day in either a foot tub with about 4 inches of warm water and about a half a cup of epsom salt, if you do the epsom salt it is good to take a calcium supplement to because the calcium helps your muscles contract, where as, the magnesium relaxes the muscles. I have also read that iron deficiency can cause mental health problems like ADHD. You really should buy some books on the topic of alternative health solutions to diseases to find out the real cause. I also highly recommend going to a Natural Doctor. Another good thing to do is get a hair analysis done to test your mineral levels, along with your toxic metal levels. It's also possibility that the Mercury poisoning and can be the cause of your mineral levels in your body to be low, which in turn can cause the symptoms too, so to counteract that, you might be able to just supplement with the minerals you need. But if you want to understand the cross and be saved by faith versus saved by default due to your mental illness then you've got to get healed of Attention-Deficit Disorder.

There are so many health problems out there associated with heavy metal poisoning. I have read that cancer could also be associated with having toxic metals in our body. I also wanted to say we need to get a bill passed that will ban these type of dental fillings and stop the use of aluminum drinking cans, and stop the use of mercury in all vaccinations so please do your part. Here is a website that gives you a list of all the Senators phone numbers so you can call and do your part it: http://www.theorator.com/senate.html By the way, when you see an alternative health doctor ask about the different chelation products. One of the main products is known as DMSA. I tried EDTA, and it didn't seem to help. EDTA is just another type of chelation therapy. I also read that 85 percent of people who get chelation therapy never get cancer in their life. I also have read testimonies of people taking zeolite and then the cancer goes away after a certain time period. I am not saying it is a cure for cancer but I have read those testimonies. Another thing is you still have to stay on these products for a while and get a urine toxic metal test after and before doing a chelation therapy to test to see how much of the toxic metals are left in your body. I am still fighting this disease of attention-deficit disorder, along with some other mental diseases. It is a long process to get better so keep me in your prayers.

So now that you know what could be causing your illness, you can do something about it. If you don't do anything and you don't have faith when you die, then realize you will still face a judgment. I'd rather be sure I have faith than take chance on getting in heaven on a technicality. It also says in **Romans 2:12-16** that those who never hear the gospel will be judged according to their conscience and if we are always striving to do the right thing and also repenting according to our conscience then we will be saved on judgment day, but remember there is no escaping judgment. But I still would rather have faith on the Day of Judgment then be judged by my conscience. Also remember the other verse I shared earlier that in **Luke 12:47-49** that if we know the Master's business and we don't do what it takes to get ready we will be beaten with many blows, and now that you have read all of this you do know the Master's business. So don't give up. Hang in there you can do it, just get help from others too.

Here is a scripture that tells us how we need to follow God in order to be worthy of this calling. **Luke 14:26** *"If anyone comes to me and does not hate (love less) father and mother, wife and children, brothers and sisters—yes, even their own life—such a person cannot be my disciple"* (NIV) In **verse 33**, *"In the same way, those of you who do not give up everything you have cannot be my disciples."* So if you are afraid of spending money to get your health in order to be saved, you can't be a disciple of Christ, at least by faith. Another verse we should consider is **Luke 9:23**; it says, *"And he said to them all, If any man will come after me, let him deny himself, and take up his cross daily, and follow me."* (King James) *Finally*, in **1 John 2:6** *"Whoever claims to live in him must live as Jesus did."* (NIV) The last thing I want to say in this chapter is there is two sides this topic of can the mentally handicapped being saved. The one side is you have to have faith in order to be saved which includes understanding and a sharp mind. The other side is that children and those like children, the mentally handicapped, belong to the Kingdom of God because they can't understand right from wrong. In **John 9:41** it says, *"If you were blind you would not be guilty of sin; but now that you claim you can see your guilt remains."* (NIV) So basically if we can't even see that we are sinners or because we can't see and understand our guilt then we are still innocent. I know I feel like I am lost all of the time because my mental sharpness is dull and my understanding and clarity isn't where it needs to be, plus I have a fear of death and that is why I wrote this chapter with the point of view that you need to be mentally sharp to be saved, but I may very well be saved because of what **John 9:41** says and because of what **Matthew 19:14** and **Luke 18:16** say. You may very well be saved too if you have the mind of a child. It is just hard to understand the way God feels about us when we can't grasp these things for ourselves.

# Notes

# Chapter 11

# Staying Saved!

The first thing we need to do in our walk with God is to make sure we are forgiven and have become a child of God. Once this has occurred, we need to ask ourselves, "What must I do to stay saved," because we can lose our salvation. I have already gone over some of these scriptures in a different context, but I will repeat them just to make sure you get the point. The main thing we must do is keep believing that Jesus has died for our sins. The Bible says we are justified by faith, which means we are right with God when we continue in our faith or belief that Jesus has paid the penalty for our sins. The scripture that backs this up is **1 Corinthians 15:2** *"By this gospel you are saved, if you hold firmly to the word I preached to you. Otherwise, you have believed in vain."* (NIV) Realize that the word "if" is used, so it is conditional on grasping firmly to the gospel message. What we need to grasp firmly to is the message that Jesus died for our sins and was buried and was resurrected from the grave. In context, it is not referring to grasping firmly to the whole New Testament, just the death, burial, and resurrection.

Another scripture that confirms this belief concept to stay saved is **Ephesians 3:17** *"So that Christ may dwell in your hearts through faith."* (NIV) So we know that Christ dwells or lives in our hearts through faith. Another scripture that is about staying saved is **Hebrews 3:6** *"But Christ is faithful as the Son over God's house. And we are his house, if indeed we hold firmly to our confidence* *and the hope in which we glory."* (NIV) So we need to hold onto courage and hope in the cross and our salvation if we want to stay saved. Also, in **Hebrews 2:1-2** *"We must pay the most careful attention, therefore, to what we have heard, so that we do not drift away."* (NIV) Drift away from what? From faith in the cross, burial, and resurrection! In **verse 3**, *"How shall we escape if we ignore so great a salvation?"* (NIV) Also, in **Hebrews 3:14**, it says, *"We have come to share in Christ, if indeed we hold our original conviction firmly to the very end."* (NIV) What does that mean? It means we must keep our conviction and faith in the cross.

What is the next thing we need to do to stay saved? We need to stay away from unrepentant sin. That means we don't deliberately live for our sin. Now we are going to fall short and sin. We may even try hard and still sin often. This is talked about by the apostle Paul in **Romans 7:14-20**

> *"For we know that the law is spiritual: but I am carnal, sold under sin.*
> *For that which I do I know not: for not what I would, that do I practise; but what I hate, that I do.*
> *But if what I would not, that I do, I consent unto the law that it is good.*
> *So now it is no more I that do it, but sin which dwelleth in me.*
> *For I know that in me, that is, in my flesh, dwelleth no good thing: for to will is present with me, but to do that which is good is not.*
> *For the good which I would I do not: but the evil which I would not, that I practise.*
> *But if what I would not, that I do, it is no more I that do it, but sin which dwelleth in me.*
> *I find then the law, that, to me who would do good, evil is present.*
> *For I delight in the law of God after the inward man:*
> *but I see a different law in my members, warring against the law of my mind, and bringing me into captivity under the law of sin which is in my members.*
> *Wretched man that I am! who shall deliver me out of the body of this death?*

*I thank God through Jesus Christ our Lord. So then I of myself with the mind, indeed, serve the law of God; but with the flesh the law of sin." (American Standard)*

This verse completely explains that we are going to try to do good, and it will be hard to carry it out, and it also says we are going to still struggle with sin and will still do evil things, but we must still stay faithful because Jesus has given us victory over the punishment of sin **(1 Cor. 15:56-57)**. We can still be saved and fall short time after time; we just can't deliberately fall short over and over without repenting. Also remember the scriptures in Nehemiah and Judges, which will teach how patient God is. Remember though that God will show you if you lost your salvation by a *"fearful expectation of judgment and of raging fire"* (NIV) **(Heb. 10:26)**.

The final thing we need to do to stay saved is we need to acknowledge our sinful nature to God as we sin because if we don't apologize to God when we sin, then are we really repenting, and we already talked about the type of repentance we need to have with godly sorrow, remember Zacchaeus. But the two scriptures that talk about acknowledging or confessing our sins to God are as follows:

**1 John 1:8-10** *"If we claim to be without sin, we deceive ourselves and the truth is not in us. If we confess our sins, he is faithful and just and will forgive us our sins and purify us from all unrighteousness. If we claim we have not sinned, we make him out to be a liar and his word is not in us."* (NIV) So you see we need to confess or acknowledge our sinfulness to God as we see it. If we have a repentant heart, we'll apologize too. If we don't confess our sins to God, then we will feel guilty, and the answer to this is to pray and ask for God's forgiveness. In **Psalms 32:5** *"Then I acknowledged my sin to you and did not cover up my iniquity. I said, "I will confess my transgressions to the Lord." And you forgave the guilt of my sin. (NIV)* According to this scripture, we need to acknowledge our sinfulness to get forgiveness, which means we don't deny the fact that we have sinned or are sinners. Obviously, we can't acknowledge every sin we commit because we can't see them all. Sometimes we might commit small sins and just not acknowledge them. I believe God still understands that we are going to forget to confess everything that we do wrong, and that is where grace kicks in. Just remember Christ dwells in our hearts by faith, and if you feel guilty, just pray to God and acknowledge your sin, and the blood of Jesus will cleanse your conscience. The last thing I want to say about this last paragraph of this chapter is that I have contemplated this topic of confessing our sins to stay saved, and I am not 100% sure that you have to confess your sins to stay saved I do believe that you need to believe that you are a sinner and confess the fact that you are a sinner, but whether or not you need to confess every time you sin is a little outrageous, because it is impossible for one thing and next it seems as if you are working to stay saved which is kind of a work of the law. Just another thing to remember is **Ephesians 3:17** which basically says that the Holy Spirit resides in our heart by faith, not by confessing sins. So I would just say examine 1 John and ask people to help you understand it better. One other thing, God will let you know if he wants you to confess your sins by disciplining you if you need to pray about it. God will also let you know if you need to pray longer, too by disciplining you more. In **Psalms 32:3-5** God was disciplining David, so I encourage you to read it so you can understand what the Lord's discipline is like.

So let's go over the things we need to continue in to stay saved. First, we need to continue to believe that Jesus has died for our sins. Next we need to stay away from unrepentant sin. We possibly need to confess our sins to God. Lastly, as I stated in Chapter 3 we need to stay in Church so that we can stay faithful, because when we leave church we usually go back to our sinful nature. I also stated in that same chapter we must remain in the vine because we can't bear fruit on our own. In regards to the Church we need to be in a Church where people are constantly encouraging you with phone calls and hanging out with you because this also keeps you faithful.

# Notes

# Chapter 12

# Finding the Right Church

  The first requirement in finding the right church is to get ourselves involved in a church that has that right doctrine on salvation. It has been my experience of visiting churches that when I go to a church that teaches false doctrine on salvation, my mind gets scrambled up and I get confused about the truth. If your current church doesn't teach the truth about salvation, maybe you should confront the leaders and teach them the truth or give them this book to borrow. We must also realize there are a lot of false teachers out there who don't want to preach the whole truth. They'll preach what is easiest to get people to believe they are saved so they can have as many members as possible, and that will keep their tithes as high as possible. We will cover a few false teachings in the next chapter.

  Another thing to be aware of is a church that preaches a lot about money, or all they preach about is evangelism. This may be a tactic to get church membership up and bring in the money, not always, but it's possible. The Bible does talk about giving money to the church, but it is supposed to be a free will offering, not something that is preached about a lot or in a compelling way. If it is being preached on in a way that is compelling you to give a lot of money, then be on guard against this. The Bible talks about not giving under compulsion. In **2 Corinthians 9:7** *"Each of you should give what you have decided in your heart to give, not reluctantly or under compulsion,"* (NIV) So if the church is trying to compel you to give your very best, or even tell you that you should give based on your gross income not your net income then it's not biblical. That is even talked about In **2 Corinthians 8:12** where it says that we are to give in accordance with what we do have not according to what we don't have. We have our net income and not our gross. They are trying to get as much from you as they can. I'm not sure why. They may or may not have impure motives. This makes me wonder if they should even give a small lesson before the offering because in a way they are trying to compel you to give more. I personally think we should just pray before we give the offering. But just be on your guard against these types of churches that try and get as much money from you as possible. I myself am leery of churches that take up more than one offering per service. They think of all kinds of ways for you to give money, it's just crazy. Now there may be some legitimate churches out there doing this, but I am just saying be careful. The church should be above reproach and what I mean is they should allow members of the church to see their accounting records, how much they are spending on everything. If church is really good they show receipts and canceled checks and even let you know how much their ministers are making.

Also, another type of church or church leader you need to be on guard against is one that preaches loud or arrogant sermons. They might be trying to intimidate you so they can get you to do whatever they want. This falls under the category of arrogance and sometimes being judgmental or self-righteous. In **Proverbs 8:13** *"To fear the Lord is to hate evil; I hate pride and arrogance, evil behavior and perverse speech."* (NIV) What is the definition of arrogance? It is a manner or attitude that claims themselves to be superior which is displayed in a overbearing way or attitude. But I recommend you look it up either online or in a few dictionaries.

The Word of God speaks about arrogance in **Psalms 5:5** *"The arrogant cannot stand in your presence. You hate all who do wrong."* (NIV) We must rid ourselves of arrogance if we want to be in the presence of God. The Word also speaks against leaders being overbearing and lording it over you. 1 **Peter 5:3** *"Not lording it over those entrusted to you, but being examples to the flock."* (NIV)

You may ask yourselves what does it mean to "lord over someone else." It means they are trying to make you do what they say; they are forcing their opinions on you and also demanding that you follow their advice. I have experienced people lording it over me and people preaching loud sermons, and what happens after many years of this happening to you the leaders that are doing this to you will eventually give them mind control over you and I have experienced that, so I had to leave that church.

The Bible does teach us though how we should teach men. It says in **Proverbs 16:21** *"The wise in heart are called discerning, and gracious words promote instruction."* (NIV) It is clear that our demeanor when preaching the truth is that we should be gentle or gracious or kind when we teach the Bible. The apostle Paul says in **1 Corinthians 4:21** *"What do you prefer? Shall I come to you with a rod of discipline, or shall I come in love and with a gentle spirit?"* (NIV) Even the apostle Paul was gentle when instructing them. Also in **Proverbs 25:15**, it says, *"and a gentle tongue can break a bone."* (NIV) What that means is that we can really go straight to someone's heart and help them to change if we are gentle when correcting them. An example of preaching in the New Testament is in **Acts 2:40**; it says, *"With many other words he warned them; and he pleaded with them, "Save yourselves from this corrupt generation.""* (NIV) In **Galatians 4:12** and in **Philippians 4:2**, the word "plead" is used. When we plead with someone to do something, we are basically begging so it is not being preached with arrogance or in such a way as commanding or lording it over. So it's obvious that we need to be in a church that teaches us with gentleness because that will attract people to the gospel. Also, being gentle is a way of saying that you love them, and you want them to make the decision for themselves, but when they are forcing you to take their advice, it means they want to be in control and they might have an ulterior motive. **Just look up in an exhaustive concordance the passages using the word gentle to get a better understanding of how God wants his word presented.** They may not be giving you the advice that is best for you; it may be the advice best for themselves depending on their motives. Beware of those who force their rules and advice on you especially when it is either intimidating or overbearing. Now there may have been some circumstances where people were more stern in their correction like when Jesus overthrew the tables because the money changers were in the temple courts which was God's place of worship and prayer and they were trying to make money there and against the self-righteous Pharisees and the false prophets, but in general Jesus was gentle trying to help people become his disciples.

Also, be careful of churches who always talk about you getting their advice. These churches sometimes have ulterior motives as well. They want to be involved in your every decision possibly because it may affect their pocket book. Don't get me wrong; the Bible does talk about getting advice, but I tell you to be careful who you get that advice from. The Bible says in **Mathew 7:15-16**

*"Watch out for false prophets. They come to you in sheep's clothing, but inwardly they are ferocious wolves. By their fruit you will recognize them."* (NIV) What it is talking about here is the fruit of their life the way they are. If they are overbearing that means they will force you to take their advice and if they are judgmental and self-righteous they will lay a guilt trip on you if you mess up or they might tell you your sin is really bad, which is arrogance. God can't dwell with these arrogant men, which talked about in **Psalm 5:5**. If they are like this you might want to find a different church that meets all of your needs even if you have to move out of the city you live in, or possibly pray about it and get others involved to help these men change.

Another thing that churches do is put rules on the people that aren't even in the Bible or make claims about themselves being the only church that is going to heaven. That is a lie. The churches that claim they are the only one going to heaven are possibly self-righteous and think they are doing more for God that anyone else. They might be evangelizing more or studying the Bible with more people or even they think because they confess their sins to another person that they are more righteous than you. Basically they are living by the law. Don't get me wrong we do need to do what the Bible says but it isn't our righteousness that saves us. They are trying to get their righteousness from the way they are living and they need to realize scripture like: **Philippians 3:3** *"For it is we who are the circumcision, we who serve God by his Spirit, who boast in Christ Jesus, and* *who put no confidence in the flesh—* (NIV). Also in **Philippians 3:9** it says *"not having a righteousness of my own that comes from the law, but that which is through faith in Christ—the righteousness that comes from God on the basis of faith."* (NIV) You don't have to be in their church to go to heaven.

Be careful of churches that say you can only date people in their church. But you've got to realize that it is ok to date people in other churches as long as they believe the same things you do about salvation and the importance of repentance and following Jesus. The reason that they don't want you dating other Christians outside of their church is because you'll leave their membership. Although it is important to date people with the same belief as you have because if they aren't trying to repent of their sins then they will lead you into sin and you might leave God.

Some of the things the church should be like is as follows: a church where the members are really laying down their lives for each other. In **1 John 3:16**, it says, *"This is how we know what love is: Jesus Christ laid down his life for us. And we ought to lay down our lives for our brothers and sisters." (NIV)* That scripture tells us how we need to really help our brothers and love them by our actions. We should serve one another too. In **Galatians 5:13**, *"You, my brothers and sisters, were called to be free. But do not use your freedom to indulge the flesh; rather, serve one another humbly in love."* (NIV) The Bible talks about in a couple of places that the greatest in the kingdom is the one who is a servant.

The next thing we should look for in a church is where all the members are devoted to the fellowship, the teaching, the breaking of bread, and to the prayer. In **Acts 2:42-46**, it says, *"They devoted themselves to the apostles' teaching and to fellowship, to the breaking of bread and to prayer. Everyone was filled with awe at the many wonders and signs performed by the apostles. All the believers were together and had everything in common. They sold property and possessions to give to anyone who had need. Every day they continued to meet together in the temple courts. They broke bread in their homes and ate together with glad and sincere hearts."* (NIV) It is obvious by **Acts 2:42-46** that these Christians lived like they were family.

What else makes a great church is fellowship time outside of your normal Sunday and mid-week service, hanging out, going to movies together, going bowling, reading the Bible together, praying together, and just spending time together whenever you can.

Another good thing churches should have is men and women who counsel you on life situations, marriage, dating relationships, money, and how to treat your Christian brothers and sisters. But when counseling, they should use the scriptures to help you and not lord it over you but should let you choose on your own whether or not to take their advice, and they shouldn't judge you if you don't take their advice either. The scripture that talks about counseling is **Colossians 1:28** *"He is the one we proclaim, admonishing and teaching everyone with all wisdom, so that we may present everyone fully mature in Christ."* (NIV)

A few of the last things important to a church is singing songs in church and evangelism and preaching messages that win souls to Christ, also having a number of teaching classes for learning opportunities about all kinds of life situations including good marriages, money, how to treat one another, dating, grief, depression, and teach a lot on the love of God. Preachers should bring you a well-rounded message, not just one type of message but all types of teaching to equip you for life.

## Notes

# Chapter 13

# What are a few false teachings about salvation?

*Praying* Jesus into your heart! This teaching is taken from the book of **Revelation 3:20** *"Here I am! I stand at the door and knock. If anyone hears my voice and opens the door, I will come in and eat with that person, and they with me."* (NIV) Basically, when it's saying I stand at the door and knock, it means Jesus has a message for us. If we are not a Christian then we need to become a Christian. If we have fallen away then we need to let him back in our hearts and this is the only time we are to pray to Jesus about coming back to live in us is if we already were Christians and left God and we wanted to have a relationship with him again, not to get the initial forgiveness. Besides that, the previous scripture says, *"You say, 'I am rich; I have acquired wealth and do not need a thing.' But you do not realize that you are wretched, pitiful, poor, blind and naked. I counsel you to buy from me gold refined in the fire, so you can become rich; and white clothes to wear, so you can cover your shameful nakedness; and salve to put on your eyes, so you can see."* (NIV) When it is talking about buying gold refined by fire so you can become rich and white clothes to wear, the gold refined by the fire is probably faith in Jesus and the white clothes to wear is the clothes of being washed in the blood of Jesus. How do I know this is because there is a verse in **1 Peter 1:7** that talks about our faith being refined by fire, and that's the only verse referring to anything being refined by fire in the New Testament. As for wearing clothes that are white, this is told in **Revelations 7:14** *"And he said, 'These are they who have come out of the great tribulation; they have washed their robes and made them white in the blood of the Lamb.'"* (NIV) Another scripture that is used to teach that you just pray Jesus into your heart is **Romans 10:9** when it talks about confessing with your mouth Jesus is Lord and believing in your heart that God raised him from the dead. The one thing we must realize is that we confess Jesus is Lord at baptism. The scriptures that back this up are **Acts 22:16, Acts 8:37** in the footnotes. You basically got to take every verse that talks about salvation and combine it with the other verses on salvation and that is how you are saved. You can't just take one verse that says all you got to do is believe, because that leaves repentance, baptism, and everything else I talked about.

Infant baptism! Babies can't confess Jesus is Lord or have faith that Jesus died for their sins. Babies can't have faith! We have already talked about that faith has to do with understanding what our inmost intelligence tells us, and who knows what a baby understands and believes and what baby can confess Jesus is Lord, like it says in **Romans 10**. Also we have found out the Kingdom of God belong to the little children.

What about original sin? Is the baby guilty of Adam's sin or even his parent's sin? This is talked about in **Ezekiel 18** says that the sins of the father are not carried to the sins of their children! **Verse 17 "He will not die for his father's sin; he will surely live. But his father will die for his own sin, because he practiced extortion, robbed his brother and did what was wrong among his people."** (NIV) In **verse 19-20**, *"Yet you ask, 'Why does the son not share the guilt of his father?' Since the son has done what is just and right and has been careful to keep all my decrees, he will surely live. The one who sins is the one who will die. The child will not share the guilt of the parent, nor will the parent share the guilt of the child."* (NIV) So babies are not guilty of Adam's sin.

Another thing about children or babies is the fact that sin is a violation of our conscience and the Mosiac Law and basically children do not know right from wrong until they get to a certain age. It says this in **Isaiah 7:15-16** *"He will be eating curds and honey when he knows enough to reject the wrong and choose the right, for before the boy knows enough to reject the wrong and choose the right,"* (NIV) In this verse it was talking about Jesus as a child not knowing right from wrong and he was without sin. So that tells me that children who don't know right from wrong are without sin.

The last thing I want to talk about is the one possible heresy or false teaching in the Bible and that is the book of James. Many people have claimed it is controversial. Some people have even said it shouldn't have been included in the Bible. But you make the decision on your own, and I will present to you the case about why many people think it is a heresy. Let's look at the controversial passage in **James 2:14**; it says that we need works also to save us: **James 2:14** *"What doth it profit, my brethren, though a man say he hath faith, and have not works? Can faith save him?"* (King James Version) What Paul teaches however and other New Testament scriptures is that we are saved by faith, and this is defined as believing what our inner intelligence tells us. The Bible also says faith comes from hearing the message. It comes from listening to the gospel. Faith is of the mind it is a mental thing. Doing good deeds is a physical action and doesn't necessarily mean you have faith. If you want to know if James is a heresy then compare it with other scriptures in the Bible like **Romans 5:9** *"Since we have been justified by his "blood"* (gruesome death), *how much more shall we be saved from God's wrath through him."* (NIV) This clearly states that it we were justified by Jesus' "gruesome death" and it also says that we are saved from God's wrath through Jesus, not ourselves.

**Romans 4:5** says that it is God who justifies the wicked. In **James 2:24**, it says, *"Ye see then how that by works a man is justified, and not by faith only."* (King James Version)What that is telling me is that we ourselves are justifying ourselves by our works.

**Romans 5:18** *"Consequently, just as one trespass resulted in condemnation for all people, so also one righteous act resulted in justi-*

*fication and life for all people."* (NIV) So it was one righteous act, not two or three; it is by faith and it is by grace. It is a free gift.

**Ephesians 2:8-9** *"For it is by grace you have been saved, through faith—and this is not from yourselves, it is the gift of God— not by works, so that no one can boast "*(NIV)

In **Romans 3:23-24** *"for all have sinned and fall short of the glory of God and all are justified freely by his grace through the redemption that came by Christ Jesus."* (NIV) The very word redemption means full payment that sets you free. If it is a full payment that means no extra deed or work is needed it is full and complete. Although the book of James says otherwise. Also, we are justified freely by his grace without works to justify us.

The last verse I want to share on this is **Romans 4:4-6** *"Now to the one who works, wages are not credited as a gift but as an obligation. However, to the one who does not work but trusts God who justifies the ungodly, their faith is credited as righteousness. David says the same thing when he speaks of the blessedness of the one to whom God credits righteousness apart from works."* (NIV) (Apart here means without.) So you see when you are doing good works to help justify yourself then your wages is no longer a gift, so that declares even our works or deeds have nothing to do with our salvation. I personally believe some false teachers put it in there. Maybe they were trying to do it so they could brag about the flesh or the works they had done for God. Also, just because we are not saved by good works doesn't mean we should not do all kinds of good deeds. The thing is when we realize Jesus was the free gift that was given by God and when realize that our works have nothing to do with our salvation that frees us up to work even harder. That is exactly what Paul taught in **1 Corinthians 15:10.**

This world is a hurting world and people need your help in many ways. I have had a number of people refuse to help me and it really hurt me and made me more bitter towards God, when you help someone either get better from their illness or with anything else it helps that person who got the help be more grateful and helps them appreciate God more, so you are fulfilling your purpose when you help others out.

There is probably one other thing, if you have a mental illness, you will have to work in order to get healed because our health isn't a gift; it is something we have to work for to stay well, but it isn't that work in itself that saves you—it is faith, repentance, and being baptized into Christ while calling on his name that saves you.

Thank you for reading this book. May God bless you on your journey along the way.

One final note, if you would like to email me to let me know what you thought of the book, feel free to. Here is my email address: ephesians415@aol.com

# Notes

# About Author

Spencer Doris started going to church 16 years ago. Someone asked him to study the bible to find out more about whether he was saved or not. He then studied the bible with his friends and got baptized in 1995. This was the beginning of a long journey. Ever since he got baptized he doubted and worried that he wasn't saved. He then proceeded to study the topic of salvation for 10 years. He couldn't understand why he couldn't grasp salvation. After studying for all those years he concluded that he had a disease that was preventing him from understanding the truth about salvation on a deeper level. He had attention and comprehension problems. Spencer then bought some alternative health books and after going through the different causes of these types illnesses it was concluded that his mercury dental fillings along with some mineral deficiencies caused his health problems. He then proceeded to have all his mercury dental fillings removed and began on a detox program. Three years later he continues to detox in hopes for a deeper relationship with God and Jesus.

www.ingramcontent.com/pod-product-compliance
Ingram Content Group UK Ltd.
Pitfield, Milton Keynes, MK11 3LW, UK
UKHW041955230426
12048UKWH00008B/354